MICHIGAN*
T
H
E
M
E
S

A Diverse People

Student Book

BY
Lynne Deur
AND
Jean Shafer

ISBN: 0-938682-38-5
Copyright © 1996 by River Road Publications, Inc. All rights reserved. No part of this book may be reproduced or utilized in any form or by any means, electronic or mechanical, including photocopying, recording, or by an information storage and retrieval system.

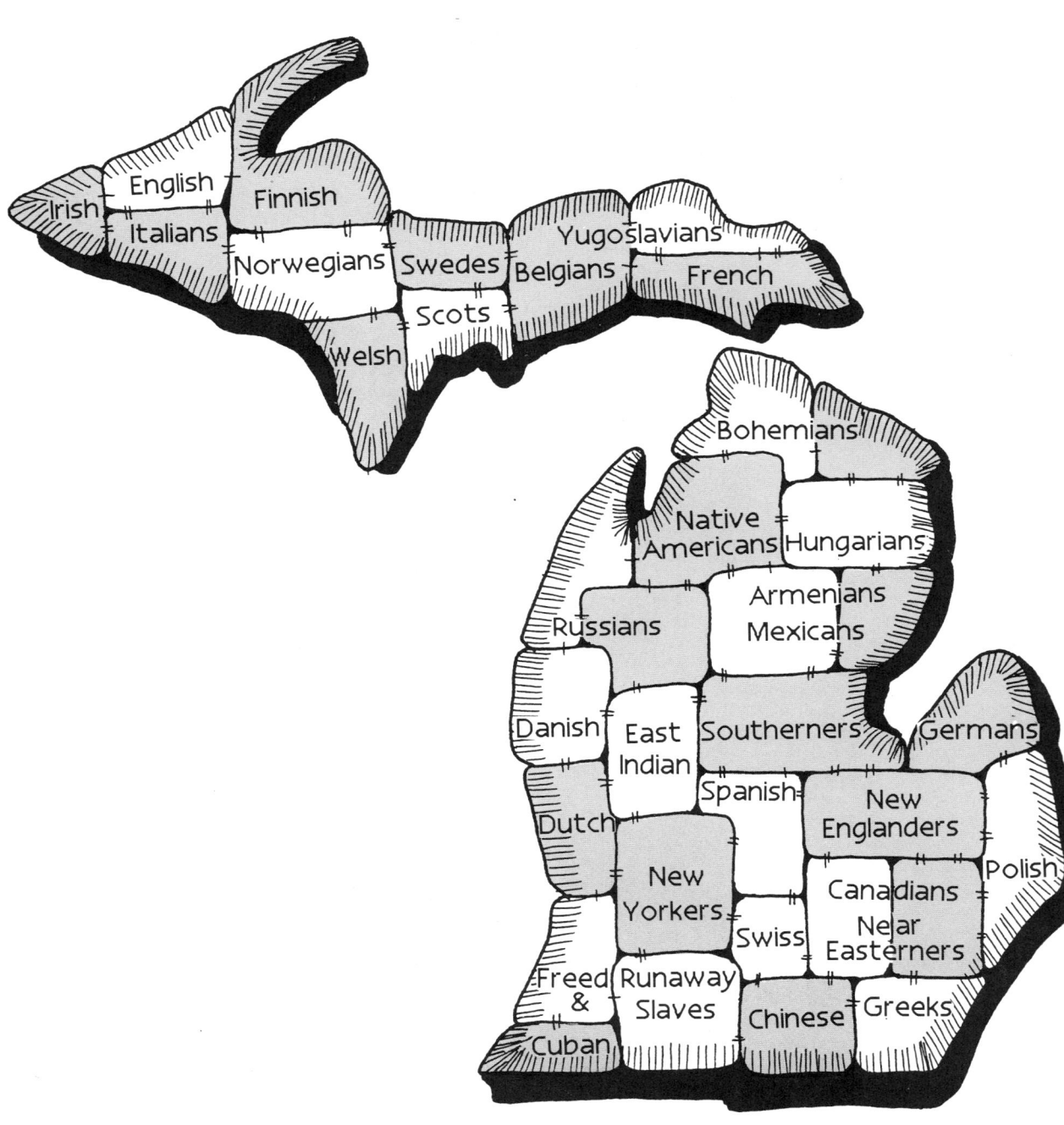

A patchwork of people

What seems to us like endless ages ago, a people we call Indians, or Native Americans, lived in what is now Michigan. The Native Americans were not a single people. They differed from group to group, often speaking different languages.

As time went by the Native Americans in the Michigan area lost their lands to people who came from other nations and also from other states within the young United States. These people came with different customs and often different languages. They created farms and towns and made Michigan a state by 1837.

But this was only the beginning. Through the years people continued to come to Michigan from all parts of the nation and the world. They came to be miners, farmers, and lumberjacks. They came to find jobs in the growing factories.

The state became like a patchwork — a patchwork of people of different races, customs, and religions. These people of many backgrounds did share one thing, however. That was the dream of finding a better life in Michigan.

The native peoples

As long as 7,000 years ago a group of people who lived in what is now Michigan's Upper Peninsula discovered how to mine copper and hammer it into tools. These tools were sharper and better than tools of stone. These Copper Culture Indians were among the first people anywhere to learn how to make them. Strangely, these people and all they knew about mining copper and making metal tools seemed to disappear. Their knowledge and skills were not passed on and improved in the centuries that followed.

About 2,000 years ago another group of people who became known as the Hopewell lived in the Michigan area. Like the Copper Culture people, the Hopewell knew how to make things from metal. They did not mine copper, but probably acquired it through trade with others who found it in old mining areas.

The Hopewell were an artistic people. They were interested in making jewelry and musical instruments, items which were purely for pleasure. They also made and decorated pottery.

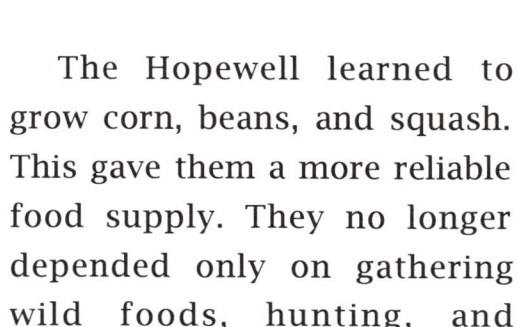

The Hopewell learned to grow corn, beans, and squash. This gave them a more reliable food supply. They no longer depended only on gathering wild foods, hunting, and fishing.

The most remarkable thing about the Hopewell were their mound-building skills. Without any machines to help them, they heaped up earth to form mounds. Some of these mounds were as high as seven-story buildings!

Over one thousand Hopewell mounds have been found in Michigan. The mounds were largely burial places, and often the Hopewell buried pottery, tools, and other objects with their dead. Experts have learned much about the lives of the Hopewell through these objects.

The Indians that met the first European explorers were not the Hopewell, but the Woodland people. Like the Hopewell, they knew how to grow beans, squash, and corn. They also depended on their hunting and fishing skills for their food.

The three main tribes in the Michigan area were the Odawa or Ottawa, the Potawatomi, and the Ojibwa who are also called Chippewa. Because these tribes were friends, they sometimes called themselves the Three Fires. Other tribes in the region

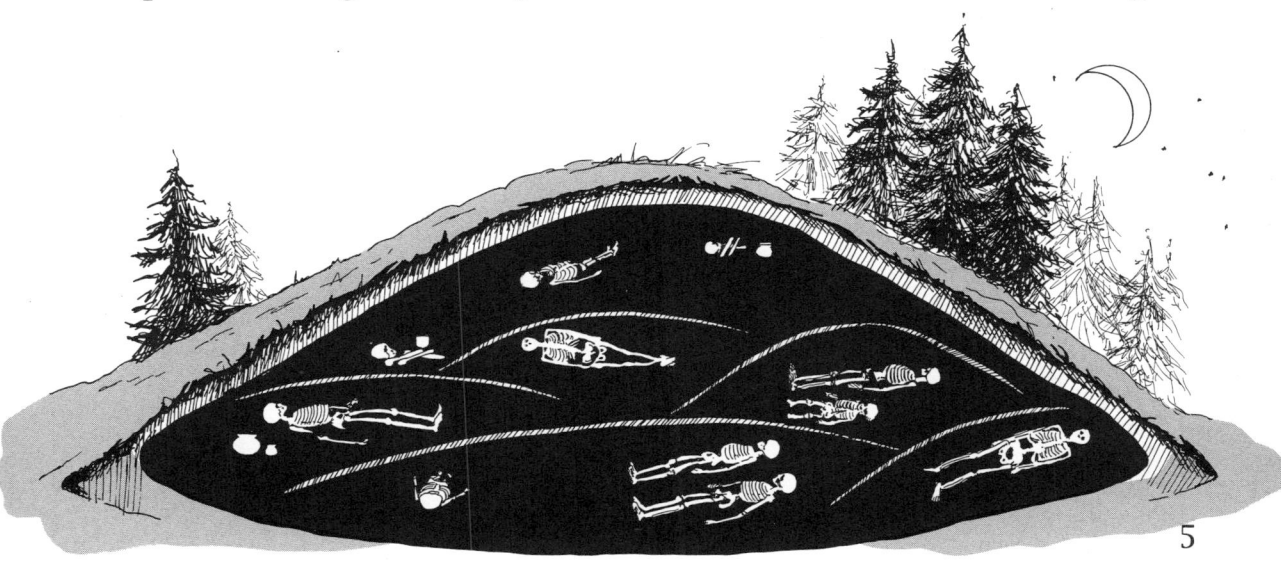

were the Menominee, the Miami, and the Huron.

Although the tribes in the Michigan area were different from each other in some ways, they also had things in common. They believed in sharing with each other. When even one hunter was successful, there would be food for all. People did not lock their wigwams, since stealing was not a problem.

All tribes believed that every living thing — from plants and animals to people — had living spirits that should be respected. It seemed to them that to take or kill more than was needed would harm everyone. They also believed that it was impossible for anyone to own the land or the lakes and rivers. Just as the sun, the moon, and the stars belong to everyone, so did the land.

The French, the British, and the Americans

The first non-Indian people in the Michigan region were the French. Some of them came looking for a waterway to the Pacific Ocean. They did not know that North America was such a huge continent. Others came to trade with the Indians for furs. Still others were priests who wanted to bring their religion to the Indians.

The French explorers, traders, and priests paddled the lakeshores and followed the Indian trails deep into the wilderness. They often wrote about their North American experiences in their journals and letters. Those writings became the first histories of the Great Lakes region.

With explorers, traders, and priests here France was able to claim a large section of North

America, including the Michigan area. But the French lost their claim after British troops defeated them in in the French and Indian War. The British then took over most of North America that had been French.

Trader

French Priest

The British also carried on fur trading in the Michigan region. In addition they had soldiers at several forts. But the British rule did not last long. America's victory in the Revolutionary War not only changed the thirteen colonies into the United States of America but also made the western Great Lakes area an American territory.

Although they lost the war, British soldiers and traders did not leave the Michigan forts. And for several years the Americans ignored them. They were busy creating a new government and rebuilding their resources after the long war. Finally, however, the Americans forced them over the border into Canada.

Americans again struggled with the British in the War of 1812. Some of the battles were fought near Detroit and on Lake Erie. Finally the Americans won the war. It settled the question forever about who really owned the Michigan region.

British Soldier

Becoming a state

The United States Congress had to make many decisions about all the unsettled land in the western Great Lakes region. They named it the Northwest Territory and debated about its future. Finally they created the Land Ordinance of 1785 and the Northwest Ordinance of 1787.

The Land Ordinance of 1785 divided the new territory into townships that were six miles square. Each township was divided into sections of 640 acres which were to be sold for at least one dollar an acre. One section in each township was to be set aside for a school.

The Northwest Ordinance of 1787 set up the rules of government for the new territory. It outlined the rules for forming new states.

In 1805 President Thomas Jefferson created the Territory of Michigan within the Northwest Territory. This new territory was not the same size and shape as today's State of Michigan. In fact, its boundaries changed on several occasions.

At first Americans did not rush to the Michigan Territory.

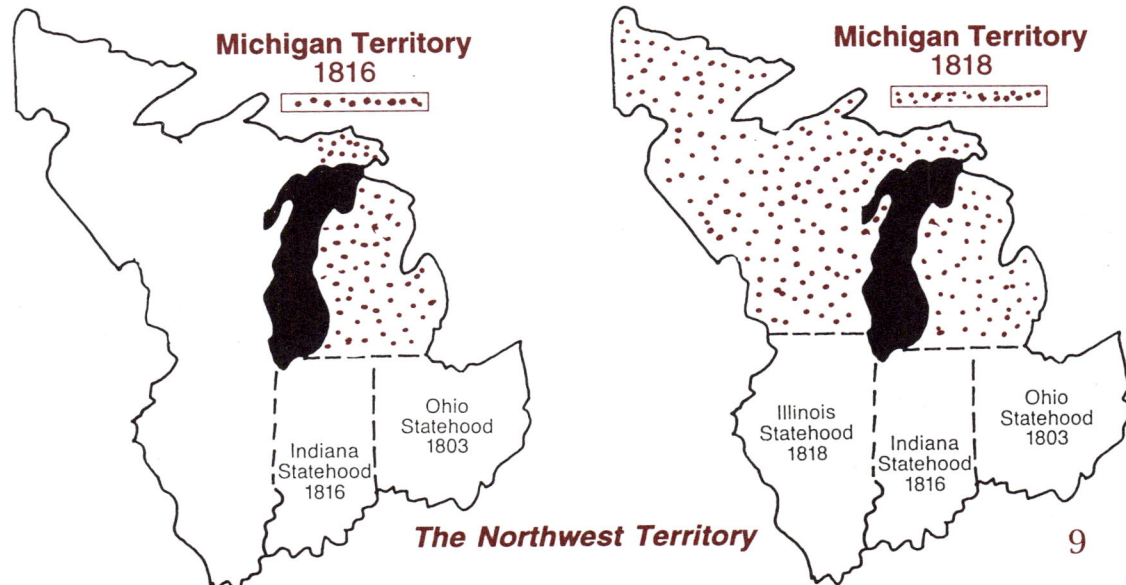

The Northwest Territory

One reason was that most of the land still really belonged to the Indian people. Lewis Cass, the first governor of the territory, set about to make treaties with the Indians so that settlement could begin.

South of the Michigan Territory there were already enough settlers to form the states of Ohio, Indiana, and Illinois. But Michigan was out of the way for settlers moving west. Many had also heard reports that its land was swampy and poor for farming.

In 1825 the history of the Michigan Territory changed with the opening of the Erie Canal in New York State. This man-made waterway created an easy and inexpensive way to travel. Settlers could take a canal boat across New York State to Buffalo. There they could board a schooner or steamship for Detroit. Large numbers of settlers began

---

MICHIGAN NEWSMAKERS
September 13, 1820

Cass Explores Territory

Territorial Governor Lewis Cass returned to Detroit today after exploring the Michigan Territory. The trip began in May and took the governor from Detroit into the northwestern part of the territory. The governor returned by canoeing south on Lake Michigan and then traveling by horseback from St. Joseph.

Cass says he has discovered many good things about the territory that are bound to encourage settlers. He has also begun making treaties with Indians so that settlement can begin. The native people seem to like Cass and call him "Big Belly."

Accompanying Cass was Henry Schoolcraft. Schoolcraft served as geologist on the trip and found traces of copper and iron ore in the northern part of the territory. Indian guides led him to a huge copper rock on the banks of the Ontonagon River. According to Governor Cass, Schoolcraft is interested in more than geology. The geologist will begin a study of Indians in the Michigan Territory in the near future.

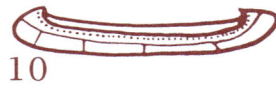

coming to Detroit and then spreading across the southern part of Michigan. Many of them were from New York State and the New England states.

By 1834 the population of Michigan had passed the 60,000 mark required for statehood. But Michigan leaders had to describe the official boundaries of their new state. That was a problem.

Michigan's survey showed that a narrow strip along its southern border, already part of the state of Ohio, really belonged to Michigan. People in Ohio, of course, did not want to give up this strip of land which included Toledo.

The argument over this little strip of land came to be known as the Toledo War, even though no battles were fought. Finally the U. S. Congress decided that Ohio should keep the strip. In exchange Michigan received a large section of the Upper Peninsula that had not been included. In 1837 President Andrew Jackson signed a bill making Michigan the sixteenth state to join the Union.

The arrival of settlers to Michigan changed the lives of its native people. President Jackson tried to force all Indian people in the eastern half of the country to move west of the Mississippi River which was still unsettled. Some of Michigan's Indians did move west during this period. Others went to live on reservations in Michigan or to remote areas in the state that settlers did not want.

MICHIGAN NEWSMAKERS
August 17, 1840

Indian Leader Stops Removal

Potawatomi leader Leopold Pokagon handed General Hugh Brady an order from a Detroit judge that stopped the removal of Pokagon's band from southwestern Michigan. Brady was under orders from President Andrew Jackson to remove all Indian people to lands west of the Mississippi River.

Pokagon had recently proved to the judge that his group had become Christian land-owning farmers who paid taxes on their land. He then argued that his band of Potawatomi should be treated like regular citizens. The judge agreed and said the group did not have to move off its land.

An Ojibwa Design

A place in the nation

Most of the people who came to settle in Michigan made a living by farming. Others worked in businesses that farmers needed. For example, some people built gristmills to grind wheat into flour or sawmills to cut logs into lumber. Others opened stores where farmers could buy supplies. Still others were ministers and teachers.

Soon other opportunities to make money brought more people to the state. Lumbering and mining became big businesses in Michigan from about 1850 to the end of the century. Thousands came to find jobs in lumber camps and iron and copper mines.

Many of Michigan's new residents were from Canada and Europe. In the mid-1800s they came from northern and western European countries such as Germany, Holland, England, Sweden, and Finland. Toward the end of the century many of the immigrants came from eastern and southern European countries such as Italy, Poland, Hungary, and Yugoslavia.

Between 1860 and 1890 over 700,000 people came to live in Michigan. Over half of them were from other countries. Although they were from different homelands, they shared a common dream. They all hoped to find a better life in America.

In 1861 people's lives were interrupted with the outbreak of the War Between the States, or the Civil War. President Abraham Lincoln called for ten military units from Michigan to help make up the Union army. State leaders had to quickly train men and outfit them for

battle. It was a hard and costly task, but Michigan was the first western state to send a company of soldiers to Washington D. C. "Thank God for Michigan," said a grateful President Lincoln.

Michigan also had a company of black soldiers. Most of these were men who had never been slaves. Some of them had been set free from slavery or were runaway slaves. A large share of these men and their families had settled in the southeastern part of the state. They were the first of many black people who eventually came to live in Michigan.

By the end of the Civil War in 1865 over 90,000 Michigan men had joined state's military companies and fought in the war. About 15,000 of them were killed. Thousands of others returned wounded or ill. Although none of the battles had taken place on Michigan soil, nearly all families were touched by the hardships, sorrow, and hatred of war.

MICHIGAN NEWSMAKERS
Lansing 1864

Woman to Work for Freed Slaves

Laura Smith Haviland was recently chosen to be a member of Michigan's Freedmen's Aid Commission. Haviland has spent the last twenty years helping freed and runaway slaves. In her new job with the commission, she will be paid to go into southern states now held by the Union armies and help the freed slaves find jobs and homes.

Haviland follows in the footsteps of another important Michigan woman. Elizabeth Chandler of Adrian helped start the Michigan Anti-Slavery Society.  Through this organization and her poetry and songs, she convinced many women to join the anti-slavery movement. Elizabeth Chandler died at a young age, some thirty years before President Abraham Lincoln proclaimed that slaves in Union-held states be freed.

A civilized place

By the time of the Civil War, Michigan was no longer a wilderness with scattered log cabins. There were towns and cities, schools and churches. Both the University of Michigan and Michigan Agricultural College (now Michigan State University) had already been established. Several smaller colleges, such as Albion, Oliviet, Hillsdale, and Adrian also had opened.

By the 1860s three major railroad systems had been built in the state. As years went by, more were added. Some of these were small and connected nearby cities. They were called interurbans and looked like streetcars. At first they were powered by steam, but later most of them ran on electricity.

As the state became more civilized, Michigan's people had time for fun. They built theaters and opera houses as far north as the mining districts of the Upper Peninsula. They enjoyed swimming, fishing, boating, and camping. By the 1880s Michigan was already known as a good place to vacation, and tourists came from Chicago and St. Louis to enjoy the state's lakeside resorts.

Near the end of the century Michigan's people were already cheering on their first sports team. The Detroit Tiger Baseball Club was formed in 1887 and became part of the American League in 1900. People in many towns in the state enjoyed the new game, along with other sports such as lawn tennis, golf, and bicycling.

The 1800s — EVERYDAY LIFE

1830s–1840s

Michigan settlers move into the wilderness, cut trees, build cabins, plant corn among the stumps and try to protect their precious farm animals from wolves.

1850

85% of Michigan's people are farmers.

Steamboats and large sailing vessels regularly carry people and products on the Great Lakes.

1860s

Michigan people can travel or ship goods by three major railroad systems in the state.

1861–1865

Michigan soldiers fight in the Civil War.

Michigan people begin to have police protection.

Kalamazoo Police Dept. — 1877
Grand Rapids Police Dept. — 1880s

N MICHIGAN — *The 1800s*

Michigan cities begin to have paid fire departments.

Detroit—1865
Grand Rapids—1871
Kalamazoo—1870s

In some Michigan cities people are enjoying a telephone in their homes.

1890s

1880s & 1890s

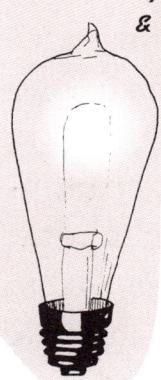

Although most people have gas lights, some are lucky enough to have new electric lights.

Bicycles win the hearts of many. New bicycle clubs begin to work for better roads.

People in Michigan's countryside can now enjoy Rural Free Delivery— or mail brought to their home.

1896

Michigan has 68,000 miles of wagon roads.
Dirt roads—poor • Gravel roads—better
Macadams*—best
*layers of broken stone & tar

The 1900s

The turn of the century brought more people to Michigan. A large number of them hoped to find jobs in the growing automobile industry which began in Michigan in the early 1900s. Some of these people were from the southern states where there were fewer factory jobs.

Just as in the 1800s, many of Michigan's new residents were immigrants. They came from countries such as Yugoslavia, Hungary, Russia, Poland, and Italy. There were also Greeks, Armenians, and Arabic-speaking peoples from Near Eastern countries. People from Finland were attracted to jobs in the auto factories as well as to the mines of Michigan's Upper Peninsula.

When the United States entered World War I (1917-1918) and World War II (1941-1945), Michigan became an even better place for people who needed jobs. During these years the auto factories were used to

---

MICHIGAN NEWSMAKERS
Detroit 1903

Olds Motor Works Is World's Largest Automobile Producer

Ransom E. Olds has created the most popular car in the world. Three thousand of the cars were produced in 1902, and it appears that production could double by 1905. The car costs $650. Olds had just created the runabout when the Detroit factory was destroyed by fire in 1891. Fortunately, a runabout was saved and has been the basis of the company's new success. The Olds Motor Works has now rebuilt its Detroit factory and created a another one in Lansing.

The popular Runabout

produce tanks, jeeps, trucks, and planes for war. Shipyards in the state were used to build warships, and Michigan mines supplied iron ore and copper for war industries.

Not only did Michigan's factories need to produce war supplies quickly, they had lost many of their usual workers. Thousands of them had joined the Army and Navy, leaving the companies with more jobs than people. Those who came to fill these jobs, including many black workers from the South, often stayed and made the state their home.

After World War II life for Michigan's people became more like it is today. In 1954 the first shopping mall opened near Detroit. Construction began on interstate highways, and in

The 1900s — EVERYDAY LIFE

Cars Change America

Michigan people are among the first to build cars and car companies.

1913

Henry Ford shocks the nation by offering auto workers $5 a day—a new high in wages.

135,000 people from Michigan serve in the armed forces in World War I.

1917–1919

1917

The average car costs $750.

Tractors are common on Michigan farms, but only 8% of farms have electricity. About 50% have telephones.

1920

1920

Women can finally vote!

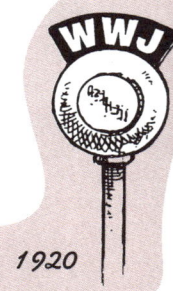

1920

Michigan has its own radio station.

N MICHIGAN — The 1900s

1927 — People can now travel to and from Detroit by airplane.

The 30s The Great Depression leaves about 1/2 of Michigan's workers without jobs. **The 30s**

600,000 Michigan men & women serve in the armed forces. Thousands of others work in factories to build war equipment.

1941–1944

1947 — People in Michigan are introduced to television!

1954 — The first shopping mall opens in Detroit.

Mackinac Bridge is completed and people can drive from the Upper Peninsula to the Lower Peninsula.

1957

1965 — Color TV becomes common.

1978 — The personal computer is invented.

1957 the Mackinac Bridge was completed. This connected the Upper and Lower Peninsulas so that cars no longer had to be loaded onto ferries in order to cross the Straits of Mackinac. Airplanes, cars, and trucks replaced railroads as the most common forms of transportation in the state. Television also began to find its place in most homes.

Although jobs have not always been plentiful in the state since World War II, Michigan's population has continued to rise. New immigrants have come from places such as China, Mexico, India, and Vietnam. Many settled in the cities around Detroit. The growing population could also be measured in cities such as Grand Rapids on the western side of the state. At the end of the twentieth century some northern cities, such as Traverse City, have also shown striking growth.

At times Michigan's diverse people have had conflicts. Race riots occurred in Michigan in 1862, 1943, and again in the 1960s. In each case, thousands of dollars worth of property was destroyed. Many people were left injured, and a few even died. Leaders in cities such as Detroit, Flint, and Grand Rapids have had to work hard to create better relations between its black and white citizens.

Michigan's patchwork of diverse people make the state an interesting place to live or visit. One can go to Holland's Tulip Festival, visit the German stores and restaurants in Frankenmuth, or eat Cornish pasties in the Upper Peninsula. There are Native American casinos for those who enjoy gambling, and Chinese and East Indian restaurants in many of the state's cities. Many groups still hold celebrations that had

their beginnings in other parts of the world.

Michigan's diverse people have helped shape a proud and interesting history. An old Michigan song tells about the growth of Michigan and its people. The first verse calls for settlers to come to the state:

> Come all ye Yankee farmer boys who would like to change your lot,
> With spunk enough to travel beyond your native spot,
> And leave behind the village where pa and ma doth stay,
> Come go with me and settle in Michigania.

Later the writer summarizes the state's growth, which had really only begun at the time this verse was written:

> What country ever grew up so great in little time,
> Just popping from a nursery right into life its prime?
> When Uncle Sam did wean her, 'twas just the other day
> And now she's quite a lady, this Michigania.

Over one hundred and fifty years after the song was written most of us could still agree that "she is quite a lady, this Michigan-i-a."